MEANING
of
HUSBANDS

Edited by
Jeffrey Young

Author: Allegra Strategies
Design: John Osborne
Researcher: Becky Hindley
Publisher: Allegra Publications Ltd

Visit our website:
meaningofeverything.com

Published by *Allegra* PUBLICATIONS Ltd © 2016

Walkden House, 10 Melton Street, London, NW1 2EB, UK

Dedicated to my father Ross

Never laugh at your wife's choices. Remember you are one of them.

My husband says he will leave me if I don't stop shopping. I am going to miss that man.

No woman has ever shot
a man while he was
washing the dishes.

Men who don't understand women fall into two categories: bachelors and husbands.

How long does it take
a man to change a
light bulb?
The months (or years) it
takes him to get off his
butt and do it.

Keep a husband seven years and he's bound to come in handy.

I love you, but I hate you.
Hug me, before I kill you.

Happy wife. Happy life.

Marriage is a relationship in which one is always right, and the other is the husband.

Men are like fine wine.
They start out as grapes.
It is our job to stamp all over
them until they mature into
something we would like
to have dinner with.

If I had my life to live over again, I would find you sooner so I could love you longer.

If my husband was half as funny as he thinks he is, he would be twice as funny as he really is.

True love isn't a big thing.
It's a million little things.

Women spend more time thinking about what men think, than men actually spend thinking.

Hardships often prepare
an ordinary person for an
extraordinary destiny.

C.S. LEWIS

Use your smile to change the world. Don't let the world change your smile.

Warning:
Marriage is the leading
cause of divorce.

Without you, I'm nothing.
With you, I'm something.
Together, we're everything.

A husband is someone who,
after taking the trash out,
gives the impression he
just cleaned the
whole house.

When you meet someone
who can cook and do
housework, don't hesitate a
minute to marry HIM.

We'd be a normal couple if
it wasn't for you.

Never make permanent
decisions on
temporary feelings.

I still miss my ex-husband,
but my aim is getting better.

Don't make me laugh, I'm trying to be mad at you.

Enjoy the little things in life, for one day you may look back and realise they were the big things.

Six words for a long
happy marriage:
Yes dear.
I'm sorry.
You're right.

When a woman says 'do whatever you want' do NOT do whatever you want.

He'll make a great
first husband.

I want a man who's kind
and understanding.
Is that too much to ask of
a millionaire?

ZSA ZSA GABOR

When it rains
look for rainbows.
When it's dark
look for stars.

Love... when your husband grabs your hand to calm you.

Single (noun): A man who makes jokes about women in the kitchen.

Ever since it started snowing my husband has been standing in front of the window and watching. If the snow gets much worse, I might let him inside the house.

Marry a man your own age
– as your beauty fades, so
will his eyesight.

PHYLLIS DILLER

Folks are usually about as happy as they make their minds up to be.

ABRAHAM LINCOLN

My wife's credit card got stolen... What a relief it was to find that the thief spends less than my wife.

You annoy me more than
I ever thought possible.
But I want to spend every
irritating minute with you.

A kiss is a lovely trick designed by nature to stop speech when words become superfluous.

INGRID BERGMAN

How you make others feel
about themselves says
a lot about you.

Not sure who are harder to raise. Husbands or kids.

The people who want to
stay in your life will
always find a way.

Ladies, if a man says he will fix it, he will. There is no need to remind him every 6 months.

Perfect men are
like unicorns.
Everybody talks
about them.
Nobody has ever
seen one.

She knew she loved him
when 'home' went from
being a place to being
a person.

ERIC MICHA'EL LEVENTHAL

Love is blind. Marriage is an eye-opener.

One kind word can change
someone's entire day.

When a woman says 'what', it's not that she didn't hear you. She's giving you a chance to change what you said.

If you want breakfast in bed, sleep in the kitchen.

When two people love each other, they don't look at each other, they look in the same direction.

GINGER ROGERS

Why are divorces
so expensive?
Because they are worth it.

It's tough to stay married.
My wife kisses the dog
on the lips, yet she won't
drink from my glass.

RODNEY DANGERFIELD

Immature love says: 'I love you because I need you.' Mature love says: 'I need you because I love you.'

ERICH FROMM

It takes a lot of courage
to forgive someone, but it
takes even more courage to
ask for forgiveness.

I didn't find out what happiness meant until I got married... and then it was too late.

I left my husband.

The canary was allergic.

Somewhere between our laughs, deep talks and little fights... I fell in love.

Marriage is a wonderful invention: then again, so is a bicycle repair kit.

BILLY CONNOLLY

The best things in life
aren't things.

ART BUCHWALD

My wife and I always compromise. I admit I'm wrong and she agrees with me.

I hate it when spellcheck changes my text to my husband from, 'I love you', to 'make your own dinner'.

You know a man is thinking about his future when he buys two cases of beer instead of one.

Your beliefs don't make
you a better person.
Your behaviour does.

SUKHRAJ S. DHILLON

A woman has to love a bad man once or twice in her life to really appreciate a good one.

After our marriage I will
let you kiss me where
nobody else has kissed me;
in Hawaii.

Behind every great
husband is an
awesome wife.

Be someone's sunshine
when their skies are grey.

Because of you, I laugh a little harder, cry a little less and smile a lot more.

By the time a man realises that maybe his father was right, he usually has a son who thinks he's wrong.

CHARLES WADSWORTH

Insanity is hereditary.
You get it from your children.

SAM LEVENSON

What are three words
guaranteed to humiliate
men everywhere?
Hold my handbag.

Never apologise for having high standards. People who really want to be in your life will rise up to meet them.

ZIAD K. ABDELNOUR

Marriage requires compromise. I tell him I need a new item and then he agrees with me.

When a man opens a car
door for his wife, it's either
a new car or a new wife.

PRINCE PHILIP

We always hold hands.
If I let go, she shops.

HENNY YOUNGMAN

It is only with the heart
that one sees rightly.
What is essential is
invisible to the eye.

THE LITTLE PRINCE,
ANTOINE DE SAINT-EXUPÉRY

Marriage is a fancy word for adopting a male child who cannot be handled by his parents anymore.

Men to the left.
Because women are
usually right.

Marriage is a workshop.
Where husband works
and wife shops...

My husband and I married for better or worse. He couldn't have done better and I couldn't have done worse!

Sometimes you have to
give up on people.
Not because you don't care,
but because they don't.

The male is a domestic animal which, if treated with firmness and kindness, can be trained to do most things.

JILLY COOPER

Love is grand.

Divorce is a hundred grand!

True love does not mean
being inseparable.
It means being separated
and nothing changes.

'Honey, I noticed the rug
needed vacuuming and
the toilets could use
some cleaning so I just
handled it.'
– said no husband, ever.

If you ever think about giving up, remember why you held on for so long.

HAYLEY WILLIAMS

A man in love is
incomplete until
he has married.
Then he's finished.

ZSA ZSA GABOR

Be a Fruit Loop in a
wonderful world of
Cheerios.

Don't wait for the perfect moment. Take the moment and make it perfect.

While creating men,
God promised women that a
good and ideal man would
be found in all corners of
the world. Then he made
the earth round.

Macho doesn't prove Mucho.

ZSA ZSA GABOR

My husband is always attractive, but he is smoking hot in those rare moments when I see him doing the dishes or folding laundry.

A man with one watch always knows what time it is. A man with two watches is never quite sure.

LEE SEGALL

Do not spoil what you have by desiring what you have not. Remember what you have now is once what you dreamed of.

EPICURUS

A successful marriage requires falling in love many times, always with the same person.

MIGNON MCLAUGHLIN

Marriage lets you annoy
one special person for the
rest of your life.

Men have only two emotions: hungry and horny. If in doubt, make him a sandwich.

Watching your husband
become a father is sexy
and wonderful.

CINDY CRAWFORD

You ask your husband to do the dishes, he suddenly has to poop...

True love is never going to sleep without resolving an argument.

For Him: You have to know
her to love her.
For Her: You have to love
him to know him.

My husband thinks I'm crazy. However, he's the one who married me.

Sometimes all I need
are your arms around me
and you telling me
it's going to be OK.

Meeting you was fate.
Being friends was a choice.
But falling in love with
you was out of my control.

How many roads must a man drive down before he admits he's lost?

Happiness often sneaks in through a door you didn't know you left open.

JOHN BARRYMORE

You have to fight through some bad days to earn the best days of your life.

For marriage to be a success, every woman and every man should have her and his own bathroom. The end.

CATHERINE ZETA-JONES

My husband has an
awesome wife.

You can close your eyes to the things you don't want to see, but you can't close your heart to the things you don't want to feel.

JOHNNY DEPP

Don't change so people will like you. Be yourself and the right people will love the real you.

In the end, we only regret the chances we didn't take.

LEWIS CARROLL

The ideal marriage is between a blind wife and a deaf husband.

Being married is like having a best friend who doesn't remember anything you say.

The things we take for granted, someone else is praying for.

Thank God someone threw
me away, so you could
pick me up.

Husbands are like fires –
they go out when they're
left unattended.

CHER

Men are like chocolate bars... they're sweet and smooth but head straight for your hips.

Falling in love is easy,
but staying in love is
very special.

Never trust a man, who when left alone in a room with a tea cosy, doesn't try it on.

BILLY CONNOLLY

Life always offers
a second chance.
It's called tomorrow.

There are two types of guys: those who pee in the shower and those who don't admit it.

We come to love not by finding a perfect person, but by learning to see an imperfect person perfectly.

SAM KEEN

The best way to get most husbands to do something is to suggest that perhaps they're too old to do it.

ANN BANCROFT

Men who have a pierced ear are better prepared for marriage – they've experienced pain and bought jewellery.

RITA RUDNER

If you don't do a lot of
stupid things when you
are young, you will not
have funny things to talk
about when you are old.

Marriage is like a deck of cards. In the beginning all you need are two hearts and a diamond. By the end, you wish you had a club and a spade.

An archaeologist is the best husband a woman can have; the older she gets the more interested he is in her.

AGATHA CHRISTIE

If I could give you one thing in life, I would give you the ability to see yourself through my eyes. Only then would you realise how special you are to me.

My ex and I divorced for
religious reasons.
He thought he was God,
and I didn't.

~~Life~~ Wife has a funny way
of proving us wrong.

Your marriage is in trouble if your wife says, 'You're only interested in one thing,' and you can't remember what it is.

Notes

Thoughts

Ideas

Schemes

Notes

Ideas

Dreams

Schemes

Notes

Thoughts

Ideas

Dreams

Schemes

Plans

Notes

Ideas

Schemes